W9-BGZ-186

Blue Banner Biography

Shakira

Rebecca Thatcher Murcia

J927 SHAKIRA

P.O. Box 196
Hockessin, Delaware 19707
Visit us on the web: www.mitchelllane.com
Comments? email us: mitchelllane@mitchelllane.com

Mitchell Lane PUBLISHERS

Printing   1   2   3   4   5   6   7   8   9

Blue Banner Biographies

Library of Congress Cataloging-in-Publication Data
Murcia, Rebecca Thatcher, 1962–
   Shakira / by Rebecca Thatcher Murcia.
     p. cm. — (Blue banner biographies)
   Includes discography (p.   ), bibliographical references (p.   ), and index.
   ISBN 978-1-58415-609-3 (library bound)
   1. Shakira—Juvenile literature. 2. Singers—Latin America—Biography—Juvenile literature.
I. Title.
ML3930.S46M87 2008
782.42164092—dc22
[B]   2007000664

ABOUT THE AUTHOR: Rebecca Thatcher Murcia graduated from the University of Massachusetts at Amherst and worked as a newspaper reporter for fifteen years. She lives with her two sons in Akron, Pennsylvania. Among her other books for Mitchell Lane Publishers are *The Civil Rights Movement, E.B. White,* and *Carl Sandburg.*

PHOTO CREDITS: Cover—Frazer Harrison/Getty Images; p. 4—Torsten Silz/AFP/Getty Images; p. 6—Johannes Eisele/AFP/Getty Images; p. 10—Gary I. Rothstein/WireImage; p. 12—Carlos Alvarez/Getty Images; p. 17—Roberto Schmidt/AFP/Getty Images; p. 18—Luis Benavides/AP Photo; p. 20—Photog/IPOL/Globe Photos; p. 22—Martin Rodriguez/AFP/Getty Images; p. 23—Carlos Alvarez/Getty Images; p. 25—Larry Busacca/WireImage; p. 26—Bryan Bedder/Getty Images; p. 27—Kevin Winter/Getty Images.

PLB

Blue Banner Biography

Shakira amazed a huge international audience with her performance at the World Cup final soccer game between France and Italy on July 9, 2006, at the Olympic Stadium in Berlin. Her stardom continued to grow in 2007 with the release of "Beautiful Liar"— a duet with Beyoncé.

"Hips Don't Lie"

A billion people were watching on television. There were 76,000 people in the stands at the Olympic Stadium in Berlin, Germany, including many celebrities and world leaders. It was July 9, 2006, and the final match of international soccer's biggest tournament, the World Cup—the most popular single sporting event in the world. France and Italy were playing for the championship. Before the game could begin, there was to be a cultural performance—maybe from an internationally famous rock band like U2, or a longstanding pop icon like Madonna?

No. The performers on the stage on that warm evening in Germany were Shakira, a Colombian singer, and Wyclef Jean, a Haitian-American with whom she had collaborated on the smash hit of the summer, "Hips Don't Lie." Shakira bounced forward among dancers clad in African garments, costumed musicians, and dozens of people carrying huge green and white spinning circles. She was wearing a red bikini top and a sheer red skirt, held low on her hips with a brightly colored sash. Her feet were—as is her custom—bare. In her strong, tuneful voice, she belted out the opening lines of "Hips Don't

Haitian-American Wyclef Jean and an African women's chorus joined Shakira on the stage for the special version of her hit song, "Hips Don't Lie."

Lie." She danced to the right side of the enormous multilevel stage and did some awe-inspiring, hip-shaking belly dance moves. "I never knew she could dance like this. She makes a man want to speak Spanish!" sang Wyclef Jean. "Shakira! Shakira!"

> **"I never knew she could dance like this. She makes a man want to speak Spanish!" sang Wyclef Jean. "Shakira! Shakira!"**

"Oh, baby, when you talk like that, you make a woman go mad," Shakira sang back. They continued to perform a special extended version of the hit song, celebrating the presence of many countries and cultures at the World Cup. Shakira raised her hands and clapped them above her head, signaling for the entire stadium to sing along. "People in the front—don't fight tonight!" chanted Wyclef Jean. As the song ended, Shakira gave a final shake of her chest, sending the bikini's tassels flying around, and gave Wyclef Jean a hug.

The Univision TV announcer yelled in delight, "Move your hips! Haiti and Colombia are also at the World Cup final!"

It was yet another dazzling performance by Shakira, who at the age of twenty-nine had reached an unusual level of international stardom. "Hips Don't Lie" had been gradually gaining popularity, but now it would become a true worldwide hit.

CHAPTER 2

A Child Full of Grace

Shakira Isabel Mebarak Ripoll was born on February 2, 1977, in Barranquilla, Colombia. Barranquilla is the capital of the Colombian province of Atlántico. It is a large, multi-cultural city on the Caribbean Sea that is famous for the huge carnival held there every February. Colombia, a nation of 45 million people at the northern end of South America, has a long history of violence and guerilla warfare, but it is also a beautiful, diverse country with many natural resources and a population full of dynamic, creative, hardworking people.

Shakira's mother, Nidia Ripoll Torrado, is Colombian. Her father, William Mebarak Chadid, was born in New York City of Lebanese parents. Shakira was the only child of her parents' marriage. Shakira's mother decided to name her daughter Shakira, which means "woman full of grace," or "grateful," because she wanted a name with the letter *k* in it to go with the last name Mebarak. Shakira's father had eight children—Lucy, Ana, Patricia, Robin, Alberto, Moises, Tonino, and Edward—from a previous marriage.

When she was just a baby, it was clear that Shakira was different. When she was eighteen months old, she knew her alphabet. When she was four years old, and already reading, Shakira's father took her to the Lebanese Social Club, where some girls were performing what is known in the United States as belly dancing, but is actually an ancient and respected art form from the Middle East. Shakira jumped onstage with the older dancers and began doing what they did. She has said that no one ever taught her how to belly dance; it was as though the ability was in her genes.

Shakira attended school at La Enseñanza. The school was operated by nuns from the Society of Mary, a large international Roman Catholic organization that views Mary, the mother of Jesus, as a model for Christian behavior. Most of the teachers liked Shakira, who was always a good student. The music teacher, however, told Shakira that she could not be in the student chorus because her voice sounded like a bleating goat! She was disappointed, but vowed to prove that the music teacher was wrong.

Shakira has said that no one ever taught her how to belly dance; it was as though the ability was in her genes.

The irony of Shakira's music teacher hating her voice should not overshadow the importance of the education she received at La Enseñanza. The nuns taught her not only reading, writing, and arithmetic, but also gave her a deep grounding in the Roman Catholic faith, a belief system that sustained her through many difficult times. Shakira also had a lot of fun at school, performing at weekly talent shows, playing hard at recess, and pretending to pay attention in class when she was really writing poetry in one of her notebooks. Outside of

Shakira's mother, Nidia, shows photographers a picture of Shakira at one year old. The press conference was held when the album Laundry Service *was released in 2001.*

school, Shakira's mother took her to modeling classes, where she learned to use makeup, pose for pictures, and walk gracefully. She also took dance, voice, and acting classes.

Shakira's home life was happy. Her older half brothers and sisters doted on her. There were always different kinds of music playing in the house. The family listened to traditional

Colombian music, as well as American popular music and music from William Mebarak's Lebanese background. Shakira's father's business as a jeweler allowed the family to live comfortably until Shakira was eight. Suddenly, the family went from living a middle-class lifestyle to barely scraping by. "My father even sold the air-conditioners," Shakira said years later. The eight-year-old child was furious at her parents. Realizing that their daughter did not understand what poverty was really like in Colombia, they took her to a park where hungry homeless kids sat around, satisfying their aching stomachs by sniffing poisonous glue. Shakira was horrified, and promised herself that one day that she would become successful at something and use her money to help poor children in Colombia. Shakira later said that she inherited important qualities from each of her parents. "I inherited the craziness and romanticism of my father and the realism of my mother," she said. "It is a mix that can be conflictive, but it works."

Shakira later said that she inherited important qualities from each of her parents. "I inherited the craziness and romanticism of my father and the realism of my mother."

It was at about that time that Shakira composed her first song, "Tus Gafas Oscuras," or "Your Dark Sunglasses." The song was about her father and the dark glasses he wore. She continued to write music as she grew older. She also liked to get together with friends to play volleyball or watch movies. She always wanted to go to parties, but her friends did not like to take her because her mother always insisted on her being home by midnight.

When Shakira first realized what it was like to live in poverty, she vowed she would help poor children in Colombia. In 2003, she became an ambassador of UNICEF (United Nations Children's Fund). Her parents, Nidia Ripoll and William Mebarak, accompanied Shakira at the ceremony.

Shakira's mother began taking her to local talent contests, where she often won the first-prize trophy. Monica Ariza, who produced a television show for children, noticed the twelve-year-old Shakira and told the head of Sony Colombia, Ciro Vargas, about her. Vargas listened to her sing a few lines from one of her songs in the hallway of a hotel in Bogotá, the capital of Colombia, and then offered her an audition at Sony. Shakira sang well at the audition and was signed to a recording contract. By then Shakira was thirteen years old. Her life would no longer be ordinary.

CHAPTER 3

Struggling to Be a Star

Shakira's first album, *Magia,* or *Magic,* had eight of her own original songs. The title cut was about the obsessive nature of young love. "I only live for you," Shakira sang in Spanish in a slow ballad style. "I don't know what magic you have made in me." The video shows Shakira with puffed-up, 1980s-style black hair. The album was not a hit, but Shakira had begun her career. She toured small Colombian towns, performing concerts with a band and a small group of backup dancers. When she was not performing, she was studying—she wanted to finish high school as soon as possible. For a year she was inseparable from her first boyfriend, Oscar Pardo. But unlike so many teenagers, Shakira never became angry and rebellious with her parents. She would spend many an afternoon sitting on the beach, looking out at the ocean and dreaming about a future in which she was a famous singer. "I always felt very sure about what I was designed for, what I was made for," she said later in a television interview.

Shakira's next album, *Peligro* (*Danger*), was not a good experience. She felt as though the men involved in producing the album did not listen to her. They wanted to shape the music to their tastes without consulting her. The album was a flop and Shakira was upset.

Despite the failure of *Peligro,* Shakira was invited to represent Colombia at the International Song Festival in Viña del Mar, Chile. She stunned the audience with a fantastic rendition of "Eres," or "You Are," in February of 1993, just as she turned sixteen. She wore an extremely short dress with a gold-fanned skirt and a black halter top, and black leather thigh-high boots. In perfect harmony with a large brass band, she belted out the Spanish lines to the song about a previous love. "You taught me the sweet emotion of falling in love," she sang. The audience loved Shakira; she won third place in the contest and was voted queen of the festival, which was broadcast throughout Latin America.

The audience loved Shakira; she won third place in the contest and was voted queen of the festival.

Returning to Colombia, Shakira decided to go in a different direction. She graduated from the Colombian equivalent of high school, then she and her mother moved to Bogotá. They began looking for work for Shakira as a model. To her surprise, Shakira was offered a role in a soap opera about a young rich woman who is in love with the wrong man. She acted in the soap opera, *El Oasis,* for almost three years. Whenever she wasn't busy studying her lines or performing for the camera, she was writing songs and composing music. She had a contract with Sony for three records, and she desperately wanted her third record to be a success.

One day, as she was riding home on the bus from the set of the *El Oasis,* the words to the song "¿Dónde Estás Corazón?" ("Where Are You, My Love?") came to her. Shakira has often said she feels that her songs are divinely inspired "faxes from God." Sony asked her to contribute one song to an album called *Nuestro Rock,* a compilation of different Colombian rock artists. She worked with a new producer, Luis Fernando Ochoa, to record "¿Dónde Estás Corazón?" and the song became a hit in Colombia.

Shakira realized that in Luis Fernando Ochoa, she had found an important ally in her struggle to make music her way. He understood her ideas and yet had many good ideas of his own. Together they began working on Shakira's third album, *Pies Descalzos,* or *Bare Feet.* Shakira's songs were, as usual, mostly about lost love, but in this third album Shakira found a new level of confidence and professionalism. She switches between having only an acoustic guitar at some moments and having a full band accompany her at others. The songs are urgent and heartfelt, and at times have a message beyond simple regret over a lost love. In "Se Quiere, Se Mata," or "One Loves, One Kills," Shakira denounces abortion, singing, "This rotten city, where what one does not want one can kill."

Shakira was nineteen when she finished with the recording. She knew that the album had to be more successful than her previous efforts. She prayed to God to let

> *Shakira was nineteen when she finished with the recording. She knew that the album had to be more successful than her previous efforts.*

the album sell a million copies. Ten months later, *Pies Descalzos* had sold a million copies just in Colombia, a figure that is very rare in a country where many citizens are too poor to spend money on music recordings.

> **Looking back, Shakira said she realized that *Pies Descalzos* would never have been so successful had it not been for the problems with her previous album.**

Looking back, Shakira said she realized that *Pies Descalzos* would never have been so successful had it not been for the problems with her previous album. "I think that if I had not met with failure in my second album, *Peligro,* I never would have reacted nor would I have had the determination to change my direction and reestablish my objectives," she said in an interview. "In other words, if the calluses on my feet hadn't hurt I never would have realized that my shoes were too tight. If I had not hit that wall, I never would have come out with my bare feet, to show myself who I really am."

Shakira toured all over Latin America with *Pies Descalzos.* She was hugely popular in Brazil, where she performed some of her songs in Portuguese. When she returned to Colombia, people were completely crazy about her. Crowd control outside her concert in Barranquilla failed, and two girls died in the crush of bodies outside the stadium. The next day, a girl who had missed the concert killed herself. Shakira was devastated by these events, and considered ending her career. She continued, however, and gave a huge concert in Bogotá, where thousands of people danced and sang along with her for two hours, despite rainy, cold weather.

Shakira arrives at the Billboard Latin Music Awards in 1999, where she won Pop Female of the Year. Over the next year, she increasingly became a figure on the red carpet at Latino-themed award shows.

Through her Barefoot Foundation, Shakira has built five schools in three cities in Colombia. The schools, such as this one in Quibdo near the Pacific coast area of Colombia, serve children who have suffered from the warfare and poverty in Colombia.

Now Shakira was wealthy and famous, but she still remembered the promise she had made to herself when she was eight years old about the street children in the Barranquilla park. She started a foundation in Colombia and began using her money and star power to build schools for children whose families had lost their homes in the fighting that has plagued Colombia for so many decades. She named it the Barefoot Foundation, and dedicated it to educating her native country's children. "Children are a country's best assets," she said in an interview on the foundation's Web site. "If we don't educate our children, if we don't tend to their basic needs, I don't think we can prosper as a nation."

She loved Colombia and Colombia loved her. But like the broken hearts in so many of Shakira's songs, it was time to move on.

Crossing Over

As Shakira flew from concert to concert on her *Pies Descalzos* tour, she kept a notebook full of poems and ideas for new songs. At one airport, a thief stole the suitcase containing her notebook. The experience made her start thinking about thieves, or *ladrones* in Spanish. She thought about how thieves come in many forms and that maybe even she was a thief, onstage singing to her audience. Eventually she wrote "¿Dónde Están los Ladrones?" ("Where Are the Thieves?"), which would be the title cut for her new album.

By this time, when reporters asked Shakira where she lived, she said she didn't know. She still owned an apartment in Bogotá, but she was working and living more in Miami, Florida, where well-known music producer Emilio Estefan had offered to help her with *Dónde Están los Ladrones?* Shakira was even bolder in her fourth album, singing in Arabic in "Ojos Así," or "Eyes Like Yours," and showing her growing anger with political officials in "Octavo Día," or "Eighth Day," in which she says, "I am not the kind of idiot who is

Emilio Estefan, the musical genius behind the success of Gloria Estefan and many other artists, helped Shakira cross over and find success in the English-speaking world. Shakira hugs Emilio at the First Annual Latin Grammy Awards.

easily convinced, but I speak the truth, which even a blind person can see."

Shakira's next tour took her to Buenos Aires, where she came across Antonio de la Rúa, son of the former president of Argentina. De la Rúa is an international lawyer based in New York City. Shakira said she was smitten from the beginning with de la Rúa's rugged good looks. However, she remained very close to her parents. One television interviewer asked her if she still lived with them, and Shakira answered, "I live with them. I travel with them. I even sleep with them if I get scared during the night!"

Another terror for Shakira was speaking English. She had studied the language a little in school, but had not really learned to speak it fluently until she moved to Miami. At first, English, with its hard sounds and words frequently ending in consonants, seemed to pose impossible problems for the young songwriter.

Shakira listened to a lot of music by Tracy Chapman, Bob Dylan, and other American lyricists and began to believe that she could also write in English. She prayed to God for a signal to show whether she should try to compose an English-language album. The music and the words to "Objection," a fiery tango-style denunciation of an unfaithful lover, came to her suddenly. She realized that she really could write in English and kept working on it. Gloria Estefan, a famous Miami singer and the wife of producer Emilio Estefan, spent time helping Shakira with her writing, but ultimately told her, "Don't change a thing."

In the fall of 2001, Sony released Shakira's single "Whenever Wherever," and soon followed with the release of her first English-language album, *Laundry Service*. "Whenever Wherever" was a popular hit, and Shakira became the first Latin American to have a fabulously successful English-language album. Shakira presented a new image with *Laundry Service*. At the album's release party, she mixed dark dreadlocks into her now-blond wavy hair and wore tight pants in a more rock-and-roll style. She toured the United States and Europe, where English fans at the famous

> *Shakira listened to a lot of music by Tracy Chapman, Bob Dylan, and other American lyricists and began to believe that she could also write in English.*

Shakira's fiancé, Antonio de la Rúa, is the son of the former president of Argentina. Rumors that the couple would marry in September of 2007 circulated heavily on the Internet in May of 2007.

Shakira has been very popular in Spain. In 2002, her fans were thrilled when she gave a concert in Madrid during her worldwide tour to present her album Laundry Service.

Wembley Stadium went wild as they swayed to the beat of Shakira's original songs, such as "Ojos Así" and "Inevitable," as well as her versions of classic rock favorites like Aerosmith's "Dude Looks Like a Lady."

Even as Shakira became an international superstar, she confessed to an interviewer from *Rolling Stone* that she was yearning for a life that was less rushed and more simple. "Having a farm with horses and planting tomatoes and onions," she said. "Those are the things I dream about now."

Oral Fixation—Not Gardens

Shakira may have been dreaming about horse farms and gardens, but during her waking hours she was working hard. She wrote more than 60 songs in 2002 and 2003 for her next album, which would be released in 2005 in two volumes: *Fijación Oral Vol. 1*, an entirely Spanish album, and *Oral Fixation Vol. 2,* a mostly English album. The album title comes from her thinking about how she loves to eat, to speak, and to sing—all with her mouth. "It's definitely my biggest source of pleasure because I enjoy conversation, kisses, singing," she told *People* magazine. "I live through my mouth."

Shakira toured for the album with spectacular success, playing to sold-out stadiums in Canada, Europe, Latin America, and Asia, including her appearance at the World Cup in July of 2006. She jetted into New York City for the Latin Grammys at Madison Square Garden, where she enlivened the ceremonies with not only her singing and dancing, but also her bold political statements. She accepted one trophy in the name of "all Latinos, especially immigrants here in the United States who are just trying to achieve their dream—that someday they receive the recognition they deserve."

She returned to Barranquilla for a huge stadium concert and the unveiling of a fifteen-foot-tall statute of her. She thanked Barranquilla for being like a mother to her. The city "formed me as a human being, as a woman, and also as an artist," she said.

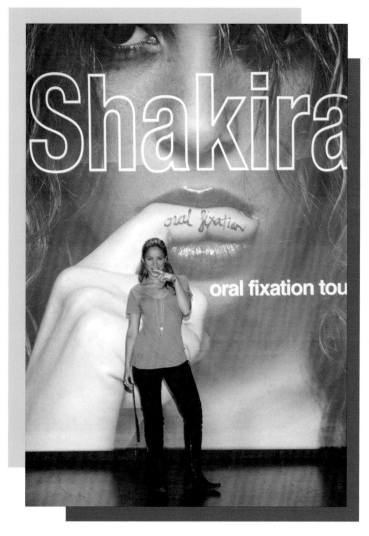

Shakira's oral fixation tour kicked off in June 2006. Earlier in the decade, Shakira had sometimes performed in nightclubs and smaller venues. But the Oral Fixation concerts were all in huge venues such as stadiums. An estimated 200,000 people attended a free concert she gave in Mexico City in May 2007.

Even as she became a megastar, she announced in November of 2006 that she planned to take some time off to study and rest. She said her fiancé, Antonio de la Rúa, had long supported her in her work, and that she wanted to take some time to support him. "Antonio has dedicated a lot of time working on my projects, he has made them his own and that is a great gift for me," she said. "Now it is time that I accompany him in the crystallization of his own."

At the 2006 Latin Grammy Awards, Shakira won four trophies. She was honored for Record of the Year, Album of the Year, Song of the Year, and Best Female Pop Vocal Album.

Shakira delighted the audience at the 49th Annual Grammy Awards in February 2007 with another smashing rendition of "Hips Don't Lie." She was nominated for an award for "Hips Don't Lie," but did not get to add a regular Grammy to her collection.

Though Shakira said she would scale back her touring, she still seemed to be everywhere. When she performed at the Grammy Awards in February 2007, the audience adored her rendition of "Hips Don't Lie." Shakira recorded a hit duet with Beyoncé, "Beautiful Liar." She made ambitious plans to give concerts in new places, such as India. She created the design for a Shakira T-shirt to be sold at Hard Rock Cafes around the world. Since Shakira is only 4 feet 11 inches tall, the shirt will be available in an extra small "ladies junior baby doll" size. She also designed the special details — including the print of a bare foot on the seats — on a European sports car that was auctioned off to raise money for her foundation.

What is without doubt is that the true Shakira—woman full of not only grace, but also wisdom, humor, and talent—will continue to emerge.

In May 2007 rumors began to fly that Shakira would marry de la Rúa in September 2007, but given the couple's fame and trouble with paparazzi, plans may be kept secret until the wedding is over. What is without doubt is that the true Shakira—woman full of not only grace, but also wisdom, humor, and talent—will continue to emerge.

1977   Shakira is born in Barranquilla, Colombia, February 2.

1990   She signs her first recording contract at the age of thirteen.

1994–
1997   She plays the role of Luisa Maria in a Colombian soap opera called *El Oasis.*

1998   She moves to Miami, and is named Latin Female Artist of the Year at the World Music Awards.

1999   She wins Pop Female of the Year at the Billboard Latin Music Awards.

2000   She wins her first two Latin Grammys.

2001   She tours Europe and the United States with *Laundry Service.*

2002   *Laundry Service* goes triple platinum.

2005   *Fijación Oral Vol. 1* and *Oral Fixation Vol. 2* are released.

2006   With Wyclef Jean, Shakira performs "Hips Don't Lie" at the FIFA (soccer) World Cup; she also wins four Latin Grammys. For her humanitarian efforts, she receives the Spirit of Hope Award at the Billboard Latin Music Awards.

2007   She performs strongly at the Grammys. Her duet with Beyoncé, "Beautiful Liar," becomes a hit.

DISCOGRAPHY

Albums

2005	*Fijación Oral Vol. 1*
	Oral Fixation Vol. 2
2004	*Live & Off the Record*
2002	*Colección de Oro*
	Shakira: Grandes Exitos
2001	*Laundry Service*
2000	*Shakira: MTV Unplugged*
1998	*¿Dónde Están los Ladrones?*
1997	*The Remixes*
1996	*Pies Descalzos*
1993	*Peligro*
1991	*Magia*

Hit Songs

2007	"Beautiful Liar" (with Beyoncé)
2006	"Hips Don't Lie"
	"Día de Enero" ("A Day in January")
	"Whenever, Wherever"
2005	"Don't Bother"
	"La Tortura" ("The Torture")
2002	"Objection"
	"Te Dejo Madrid" ("I Leave You Madrid")
	"Underneath Your Clothes"
1999	"Moscas en la Casa" ("Flies in the House")
	"Ojos Asi" ("Eyes Like Yours")

FURTHER READING

For Young Readers

Burns, Zena. "Shakira: It's Not My Hobby to Show My Belly." *Teen People.* May 2006.

Diego, Ximena. *Shakira: Woman Full of Grace.* New York: Fireside, 2001.

Rivera, Ursula. *Shakira.* Danbury, Connecticut: Children's Press, 2003.

Works Consulted

Deevoy, Adrian. "Colombian Gold." *Blender.* April/May 2002.

Du Lac, J. Freedom. "In Any Language, a Whole Lotta Shakira Goin' On." *The Washington Post.* August 13, 2006.

Gell, Aaron. "Love in the Time of Shakira." *Elle.* April 2006.

Levin, Jordan. "Colombian Singing Star Shakira Offers New Take on Life and Love." *The Miami Herald.* June 3, 2005.

Levin, Jordan. "Second Time Around, Shakira a True Superstar." *The Miami Herald.* September 16, 2006.

Millar, Cameron. "Shakira; Diva Set on World Domination." *Daily Star.* August 5, 2006.

Orwall, Bruce. "Latin Translation: Colombian Pop Star Taps American Taste in Repackaged Imports." *Wall Street Journal.* February 13, 2001.

Perry, Simon. "Oral History." *People.* December 19, 2005.

"Shakira Shaking It to Help Build School." *Associated Press.* November 6, 2006

Udovitch, Mim. "Shakira." *Rolling Stone.* October 31, 2002.

Web Addresses

Barefoot Foundation
    http://www.fundacionpiesdescalzos.com/english/index.php
Shakira
    http://www.shakira.com
Shakira Media
    http://www.shakiramedia.com
Shakira: Oral Fixation Tour
    http://www.shakiraconcerts.com

INDEX